Kid and the Terrible Truth

STEPHEN ELBOZ

Illustrated by Judy Brown

OXFORD
UNIVERSITY PRESS

OXFORD
UNIVERSITY PRESS

Great Clarendon Street, Oxford OX2 6DP

Oxford University Press is a department of the University of Oxford.
It furthers the University's objective of excellence in research, scholarship,
and education by publishing worldwide in

Oxford New York

Athens Auckland Bangkok Bogotá Buenos Aires Calcutta
Cape Town Chennai Dar es Salaam Delhi Florence Hong Kong Istanbul
Karachi Kuala Lumpur Madrid Melbourne Mexico City Mumbai
Nairobi Paris São Paulo Singapore Taipei Tokyo Toronto Warsaw

with associated companies in Berlin Ibadan

Oxford is a registered trade mark of Oxford University Press
in the UK and in certain other countries

ISBN 0 19 918686 3

Printed in Great Britain

Illustrations by Judy Brown

For my niece Nicole

Chapter One

Kid Wonder, youngest superhero in the world, was patrolling the night sky over Baggem City.

As usual, she was being watched by her proud grandpa from his room at Haddit House – home for retired superheroes.

Kid Wonder flew.

Grandpa watched.

The city was oddly silent.

At midnight, Kid Wonder returned to Haddit House.

'It's strange, Grandpa,' said Kid Wonder with a sigh, 'I've never known the city so quiet. It's like all the cat-burglars are cat-napping and the sneak-thieves are snoozing.'

'Well, you'd better get yourself off to bed too,' said Grandpa. But he was worried. He knew crime never sleeps.

And he was right. Look what was
happening over at the city prison.

Oh, help! It was a break-out. The Slippery Shadow and his gang were escaping. Oh, double help!

Now nobody in Baggem City would be safe from the greedy, grasping gang, because the Slippery Shadow had come up with a brilliant plan.

The next day, Kid Wonder went off to school. Of course, she was not wearing her Kid Wonder costume and everyone thought she was just an ordinary schoolgirl. Suddenly, her pencil-sharpener began to flash.

Kid Wonder frowned. This was serious. It would mean missing play-time. Picking up her pen, she pushed the top.

Oops, wrong pen. She picked up the right one – the one with the radio.

Up – up and away!
Whoosh!
From streets and windows, people looked up and saw Kid Wonder zoom by. They shook their heads and wondered what great crime had taken place in their city that day.

Chapter Two

Down at City Hall, Police Chief McGrabbem looked very grim.

'It's worse than we thought, Kid Wonder,' he said. 'The Slippery Shadow has kidnapped Professor Von Klimpt.'

Professor Von Klimpt was a world famous inventor. He had invented a night-time sundial,

and exercise shoes for lazy people,

and post-boxes that licked your stamps for you.

When he was kidnapped, he was working on a special kind of toothpaste that tasted of sausages and ice-cream. No one could resist it. It made you want to clean your teeth all the time.

Just when Kid Wonder and Chief McGrabbem were looking so glum they could have won first prize in a glum contest, the telephone rang. They both jumped.

Chief McGrabbem picked it up. 'Hello.'

Kid Wonder listened. Was it anything to do with the escaped gang?

'What's that?' said the police chief suddenly. 'All the city's truth drug has been stolen? It'll have to wait. I'm far too busy at the moment.'

But Kid Wonder thought the news was too important to wait.

'What does the truth drug do?' she asked.

'It forces you to give an honest answer,' replied Chief McGrabbem. 'No matter how hard you try to fib, you just can't.'

'Just a minute,' cried Kid Wonder, jumping up. 'What would you get if you mixed the stolen truth drug with the professor's toothpaste?'

Chapter Three

Meanwhile, out on the streets of Baggem City, the Slippery Shadow and his gang were hard at work.

They put up posters advertising Truthpaste. This made it difficult to resist buying the toothpaste.

Soon Truthpaste was going home in
shopping baskets all over Baggem City.

Hundreds of innocent people began brushing their teeth with Truthpaste, thinking it was just ordinary toothpaste.

The truth drug started working – immediately.

The Slippery Shadow Gang saw what they had done and could not hide their delight.

The only place where Truthpaste hadn't had any effect was Haddit House, home for retired superheroes.

There was one simple reason for this. None of the residents had any teeth.

Kid Wonder paid a special visit to her grandpa. 'This is terrible, Grandpa,' she said. 'Next week Prince Pharong-Pharong of Q'cumba is paying a special visit to Baggem City.'

'And why is that so bad, child?' asked Grandpa.

'Well …' said Kid Wonder, 'I've heard he has the most enormous nose imaginable.'

'How big is it?' asked Grandpa. 'This big?'

'Bigger,' said Kid Wonder.

'This big?'

'Bigger,' said Kid Wonder.

'Surely not,' said Grandpa, raising his eyebrows in disbelief.

'This big!' said Kid Wonder.

'Wow!' said Grandpa, 'that's not a nose to be sniffed at,' and he wheezed with laughter.

'Be serious, Grandpa,' said Kid Wonder. 'If the people have brushed their teeth in Truthpaste, they're bound to say something truthful about Prince Pharong-Pharong's enormous nose. It may well insult him.'

Possible insults to a visiting prince with a big nose:

- Brontasaurus Beak
- Concorde Snout
- King Conk
- Super Hooter
- Fin Face

(And you can think of your own.)

Kid Wonder knew that if the prince was insulted, it could lead to a war with his country.

She had to catch the Slippery Shadow Gang and quickly! But where should she start looking?

Then Grandpa had an idea.

He got an old map out of the drawer and spread it in front of Kid Wonder. He pointed at the old toothpaste factory.

'It's been standing empty for years,' he said.

Chapter Four

The old toothpaste factory was
boarded up. Its doors were chained.
It looked quite empty and half-fallen
down.

Flying high above it, Kid Wonder
looked down through her super-spy
goggles. Suddenly, something caught
her eye. *Hmm, what's that?* she
wondered.

When Kid Wonder landed, she looked at it more closely and picked it up.

Was it ordinary toothpaste – or Truthpaste? There was only one way to find out. She'd have to taste it!

She squeezed the tiniest bit on to her little finger and put it into her mouth.

Then she tried to say, 'I love Brussels sprouts, they're yummy.' But all that came out was, 'I hate Brussels sprouts, they're yucky – I hate Brussels sprouts, they're yucky.'

She simply couldn't say anything else. No matter how hard she tried, she was unable to fib.

Just then she heard a noise. Kid Wonder turned pale.

She saw a big, dark shadow appear.
The shadow grew and grew, until it
was the size of a grizzly bear. Its arms
reached out to grab her. Then she
heard a voice.

Who's there?

It didn't sound at all friendly, but
Kid Wonder was a superhero and
superheroes are always prepared for
anything.

She pressed a button on her
wonder-belt, and out flew a rope.

'Oi! I suppose you think that's funny?' said the voice. Kid Wonder smiled to herself. The rope had found him. It was Baby-Face Brewster, one of the Shadow Gang. He was on look-out duty.

'Where's the Slippery Shadow and Professor Von Klimpt?' said Kid Wonder, sternly.

'Can't tell you!' whined Baby-Face Brewster. And like a record stuck in its groove, Baby-Face Brewster wouldn't say anything else.

Kid Wonder squeezed the tube
of Truthpaste as hard as she could.
A white worm flew from its end.

The effect was amazing.

'Can't te… they're upstairs on the
top floor.'

'Thanks, Baby-Face,' grinned Kid
Wonder.

Baby-Face gave a moan. 'Oh, that
was so, so sneaky.'

Chapter Five

Kid Wonder flew to the top of the old toothpaste factory and peered through a dirty, cracked window.

She could see Professor Von Klimpt, tied to a chair.

The Slippery Shadow was giving orders to his gang.

'Let's get those tubes of Truthpaste packed and sent out to the supermarkets. As soon as everyone starts telling Prince Pharong-Pharong how big his nose is, he'll be so insulted, he'll declare war. Then we can start selling exploding custard tarts to both sides. We'll make loads of money!'

So that's Slippery's plan, is it? thought Kid Wonder. *Time for action.*

She noticed something near the window.

Reaching through the broken glass, she squirted the last of the Truthpaste into the teapot.

She was just in time.

'Tea up, my fellow villains!' cried the Slippery Shadow.

As Kid Wonder watched, the Slippery Shadow and his gang slurped their tea.

They seemed very pleased with themselves, but not for long. A few seconds later, things quickly began to change.

'Yuk!' said Fingers O'Brien. 'Who made this muck? Was it you, Squeaky? I've always hated your tea.'

Squeaky Malloy narrowed his eyes. 'Well, I think *your* tea tastes as if you use old socks instead of tea-bags!'

'Shut up, both of you!' roared the Slippery Shadow. 'This stupid bickering really gets on my nerves. You're like school kids at times!'

In next to no time, the gang was fighting among itself.

'Good,' said Kid Wonder. 'Give them
a taste of their own medicine – or do I
mean Truthpaste?'

She climbed through the window and untied Professor Von Klimpt. He was busy planning a machine for rescuing kidnapped people. He didn't even notice her.

Nose for sniffing out kidnappers

Flashing light so the kidnappers think the police have arrived

Loudspeakers for making a noise like an angry dog

Scissors for cutting rope around the tied up person

Battering ram for knocking down walls and doors

Computer which knows all the hiding places

And he didn't notice, either, when Kid Wonder used her superhuman strength to pick him up and fly him to City Hall.

'For such a brain box,' sighed Kid Wonder, 'he doesn't notice much at all.'

Chapter Six

Police Chief McGrabbem leaned back in his chair and smiled with delight.

'Well done, Kid Wonder,' he said, 'now we can go and nab the gang.'

'Not yet, Chief,' said Kid Wonder, 'I have a plan.' And she whispered in his ear.

With that she was gone.

Back at the old toothpaste factory, the gang was still squabbling.

Nobody noticed Kid Wonder return. And nobody was watching the machine that was churning out the tubes of Truthpaste, so ...

Kid Wonder pulled the control lever as far across as it would go.

The machine clanked, hissed, gasped, groaned and rumbled, and went faster and faster and faster.

The pile of Truthpaste grew bigger and bigger and bigger until, under its own weight, caps began to burst off.

Truthpaste exploded in all directions and a great gush of sticky white Truthpaste swept over the gang.

At last the squabbling ended! The gang looked like melting snowmen.

We've been well and truly pasted.

We've gone own the tube this time.

I suppose you'd call this a sticky end.

Kid Wonder stepped from behind the machine.

'Do you give yourselves up?' she demanded.

The Slippery Shadow knew he had been outsmarted. What choice had he but to surrender?

The gang put up their hands.

A few minutes later, Police Chief McGrabbem and his men burst in. 'Take them away and lock them up, boys,' ordered the police chief, sternly.

Four sets of hand cuffs clicked and the gang was led away.

'But we'll be back, Kid Wonder, we'll be back!' the Slippery Shadow growled.

Chapter Seven

The day of the visit of Prince Pharong-Pharong of Q'cumba finally arrived.

'I'm going to make a little speech,' said Chief McGrabbem.

'Er … how nice,' said Kid Wonder. And she thought, *It's a good job I haven't cleaned my teeth with Truthpaste!*

Everybody waited at the city airport for the prince's plane to land.

The plane's door opened and out stepped the prince. Or rather his nose did. And it kept on coming and coming.

At last the prince appeared on the end of it, like a sausage on a cocktail stick.

Everyone wanted to gasp when they saw the size of the prince's nose. But they were so polite that they mentioned every subject, except the one sticking out from the prince's face.

The reporter from the *Daily Comet* asked the prince if it was true that he owned a pack of white tigers.

The reporter from Channel News wanted to know about the prince's golden palace.

Cameras flashed and reporters scribbled with their pencils.

No one even glanced at the prince's nose. All went well until Chief McGrabbem stood up to make his speech.

'As everyone in Baggem City knows – sorry – sorry, I didn't mean *nose*. That is, not the big thing in the middle of your face. Not that you have a big nose, your Bigness – I mean Highness. Well, I suppose it might be a trifle larger than usual. My *point* is, your Snozzleship. Not that anyone could ever claim your nose was pointed – even though it is. Oh blow it! Not your nose, your Snoutship. I mean …
I mean … *Help!*'

Everyone was horrified. What was the prince going to say?

Slowly the prince rose to his feet.

And he smiled. 'At last!' he said.
'Somebody has noticed my nose. I
thought you must be blind to miss it,
and I am particularly proud of my
beautiful nose.'

There were relieved smiles all round.
At City Hall a party was given in the
prince's honour. It was considered a
great success.

Afterwards, Kid Wonder pushed her grandpa back to Haddit House. She thought about all that had happened that day.

'You know what, Grandpa,' she said at last, 'what I can't understand is, sometimes you get in trouble if you don't tell the truth, and sometimes you get in trouble if you do. I don't think I'll ever understand grown-ups and their ways.'

Grandpa smiled to himself. 'Nor me, Kid Wonder, nor me. Heh-heh-heh.'

About the author

When I was young
I was never interested
in Batman and
Superman. I thought
them far too serious
and much preferred
cartoon characters
who made me
laugh. But then I thought, why
couldn't a superhero be funny as well
as fight crime? I grabbed my pencil –
my story had arrived …

Apart from being a writer, I am a
teacher in Corby, Northants; and I do
find it quite a thrill when I see anyone
reading a book of mine.

Other Treetops books at this level include:
Dads Win Prizes by Debbie White
Scrapman and Scrapcat by Carolyn Bear
Me and My Newt by Pippa Goodhart
Doohickey and the Robot by Jonathan Emmett
A Kitten in Daisy Street by Pat Belford

Also available in packs
Stage 12+ pack D   0 19 918688 X
Stage 12+ class pack D   0 19 918689 8